The "Let's Review!" pages at the end of each section help reinforce learning.

The "More to Know" section at the end of the book provides additional information to help you understand the subject.

Index Quickly find the word you're looking for with the index at the end of the book.

Look for the colored boxes in the bottom right-hand corners. You will find references to related subjects in other parts of the book.

KT-469-805

Types of
Dinosaurs

🦖 Ancient Reptiles

Did you know all dinosaurs are reptiles? They ranged in size from ones as tall as a five-story building to those that were the size of chickens. Some had spikes, others had horns, and many even had feathers.

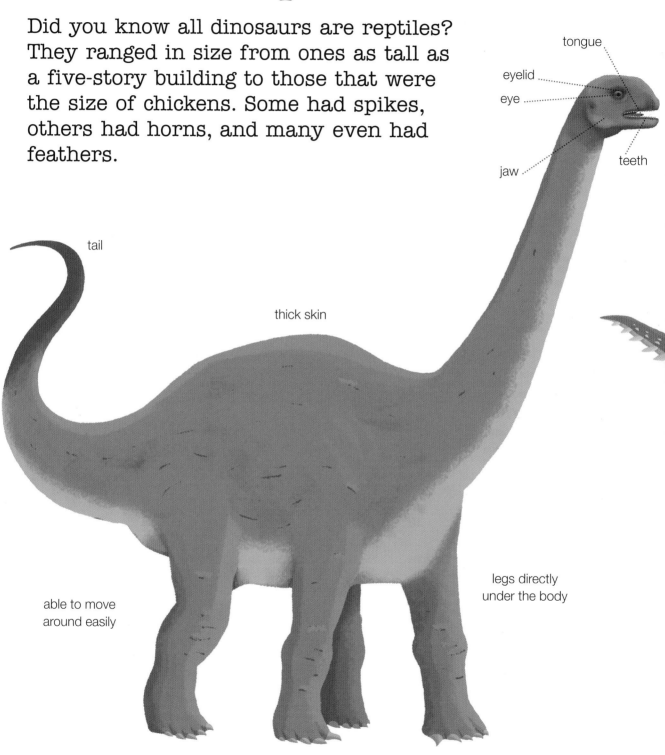

tongue

eyelid

eye

jaw

teeth

tail

thick skin

able to move around easily

legs directly under the body

Vulcanodon

crest

teeth

tail

claws

Guanlong

crest

neck

beak

Lambeosaurus

spikes

Gastonia

thick skin

frill

horn

Centrosaurus

sail

Spinosaurus

Dinosaurs lived between 230 million and 66 million years ago, long before humans.

Over millions of years, different species existed. Some lived in the same time period, while others came before or after them.

For example, by the time the Tyrannosaurus appeared, the Diplodocus didn't exist anymore. They never met.

🖼 The First Dinosaurs

Dinosaurs appeared at the end of a prehistoric time period called the Triassic, about 230 million years ago.

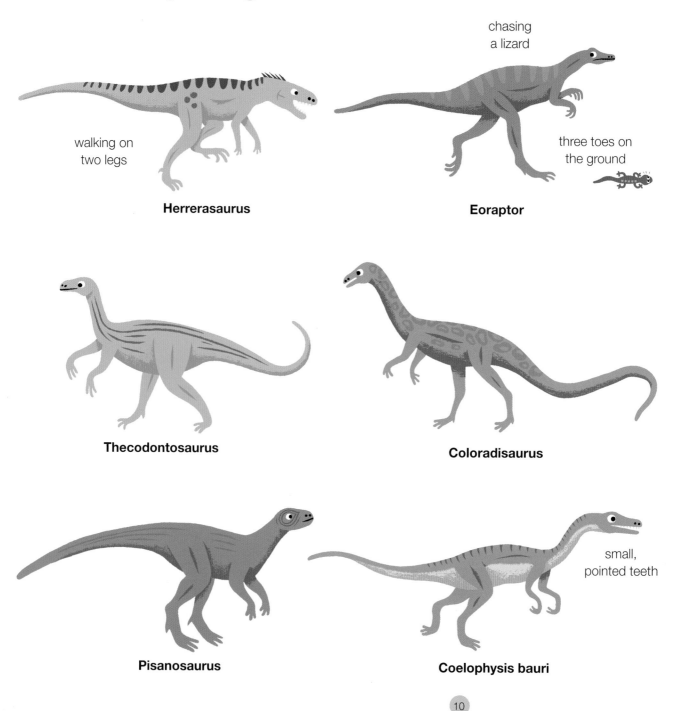

chasing a lizard

walking on two legs

three toes on the ground

Herrerasaurus

Eoraptor

Thecodontosaurus

Coloradisaurus

small, pointed teeth

Pisanosaurus

Coelophysis bauri

long fingers
with claws

Plateosaurus

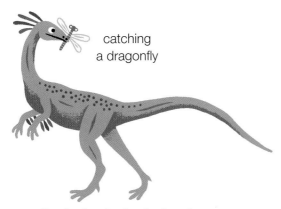

catching
a dragonfly

Coelophysis rhodesiensis

small head

walking on
four legs

Melanorosaurus

In the time of the dinosaurs, there was only one really large land mass. That land, over time, split into several pieces that we now know as continents.

Dinosaurs could be found pretty much everywhere. But some of them lived only in certain regions.

Imagine: A long time ago, dinosaurs might have lived where you live now. Have dinosaur bones been found near you?

From Past to Present **82**
The World of Dinosaurs **88**

Theropods

These predatory dinosaurs moved around on two legs and sometimes even flew. They were fearsome!

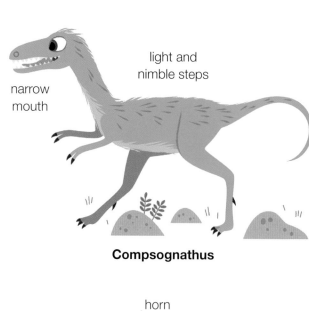

narrow mouth

light and nimble steps

Compsognathus

powerful hind legs

Tyrannosaurus

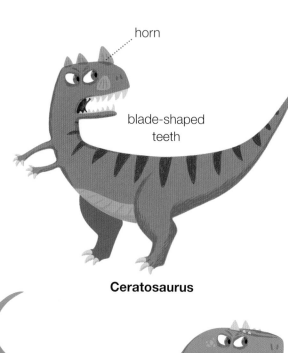

horn

blade-shaped teeth

Ceratosaurus

very sturdy head

Albertosaurus

eating a big chunk of meat

Allosaurus

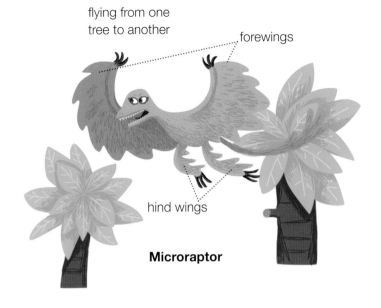

flying from one
tree to another

forewings

hind wings

Microraptor

Deinonychus

huge claws

crest

sharp,
toothless
beak

Oviraptor

Some theropods were very big: The Tyrannosaurus was as tall as 15 children your age!

But they came in all sizes: Some were as small as a chicken, some were as big as humans, and some were as tall as a one-story house.

Watch out! The little ones could be very dangerous too. The Deinonychus was no bigger than you, but it was especially aggressive.

🌴 Sauropods

These giants were some of the biggest living creatures to ever exist.

nostril

walking
on four legs

Dicraeosaurus

small, elongated
head

long neck

eating
leaves

about 70 feet (21 meters)
long from head to tail

claws

Apatosaurus

small, peg-like teeth

long tail that can snap like a whip

neck that was 30 feet (9 meters) long

Mamenchisaurus

Some sauropods were as long as four city buses. Next to them, you'd look almost as small as an ant.

The sauropods' large size and strength intimidated their enemies, who were hesitant to attack them.

Sauropods were actually rather peaceful and ate only plants. They moved slowly because they were so heavy.

Thyreophorans

Plates, spikes, or armor made of bone protected these hefty dinosaurs!

double row of spiky plates on the back

tail spikes

neck spikes

eating a fern

Huayangosaurus

spikes

club-shaped tail

Talarurus

armor

eating plants
on the ground

Panoplosaurus

tail spikes

Kentrosaurus

bony plates

escaping into
a bush

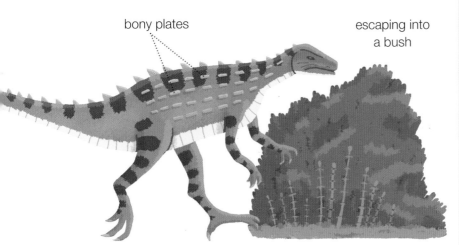

Scutellosaurus

Dragons in stories are imaginary
reptiles that never existed.
Dinosaurs actually lived on Earth.

During their time, dinosaurs
made up a large population
of huge beasts on Earth.
But they never breathed fire!

Just as imaginary dragons have
nothing to do with dinosaurs,
some real animals today aren't
related, either—even though
they may look like dinosaurs!

After the Dinosaurs **70**

Ornithopods

These plant-eaters walked on four legs . . .
but ran on two!

fan-shaped sail

duck bill

Ouranosaurus

Iguanodon

small crest

duck bill

sitting on eggs
in a nest

Maiasaura

hundreds of tightly packed little teeth

duck bill

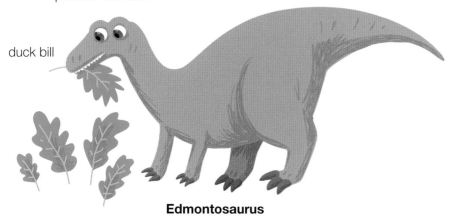

Edmontosaurus

long, muscular legs

five digits

Dryosaurus

Scientists have studied the shapes and sizes of dinosaurs. They have also found out the exact color of some of them!

Scientists use fossil bones, eggs, footprints, and even the fossilized skin and feathers of dinosaurs to figure out their colors.

Where dinosaurs lived and how they spent their time also provide clues to their colors.

Marginocephalians

Their sturdy heads sported bumps, horns, or a big, tough collar called a frill.

bony skullcap

adult
Pachycephalosaurus

horns

bony skullcap

row of spikes

young
Pachycephalosaurus

bristles

cheek bumps

parrotlike beak

long hind legs

Psittacosaurus

bump

Leptoceratops

Compared with theirs, your head is very small! It must have been difficult for their necks to support all those heavy bumps.

frill

powerful beak

Protoceratops

Scientists think these dinosaurs used their skull features for protection, fighting, and showing off.

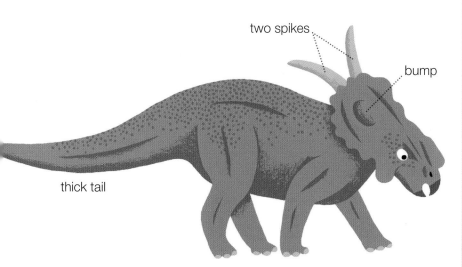

two spikes

bump

thick tail

Achelousaurus

Can you think of any animals today that have similar sturdy protection and look a little like these dinosaurs?

Triceratops **30**
Reproduction **54**

Let's Review!

Which dinosaurs walked on their two hind legs? Which ones were very large? Which ones had plates and spikes on their bodies? Which ones had big, sturdy heads?

In these pictures of dinosaur body parts, find:

a horn

a foot

spikes

a crest

teeth

a frill

a beak

Use your finger to trace a line between each dinosaur's head and its whole body.

Which of these dinosaurs is your favorite? Why?

Popular
Dinosaurs

Diplodocus

One of the best-known sauropods, this plant-eater lived toward the end of the Jurassic period.

sequoia

cycads

wading in the water

araucaria

lowering its head to drink

living in a herd

dorsal spines

walking slowly

big eyes

very small head

small teeth arranged like a comb

broad claws

big feet

fern

grazing on tender plants

Why were their necks and tails so long ?

facing danger

Ceratosaurus

long, thin, flexible tail

young Diplodocus

horsetail

You can easily recognize a Diplodocus: Its elongated neck and tail look like tubes! And it has a big, round belly.

The long neck of this dinosaur allowed it to reach plants far to the side or down low. It used its long tail for balance.

The Diplodocus also used its tail to strike enemies and maybe to express itself by cracking it like a whip. How do other animals use their tails?

Tyrannosaurus

This meat-eating theropod lived about 68 million years ago in what is now western North America.

eating already-dead prey

oak tree

smelling a dead animal's trail

strong neck

huge head

powerful jaws

very long, sharp teeth

short tongue

a sick Edmontosaurus

hunting

lying in wait
for prey

tail upright
for balance

muscular
thigh

two small
forelegs

two clawed
fingers

magnolia

Why

are they always the bad guys in movies

?

When you see a Tyrannosaurus in a movie or cartoon, you tremble with fear. Even adults get scared!

It was huge, it had very sharp teeth, and it could have swallowed a human. Unbeatable and merciless: the perfect villain!

Its body was made for hunting because the Tyrannosaurus had to eat meat to live. Can you name other animals that hunt?

Triceratops

This stocky plant-eater was part of a group of dinosaurs called ceratopsians. It had front-facing horns and a thick frill that protected its neck.

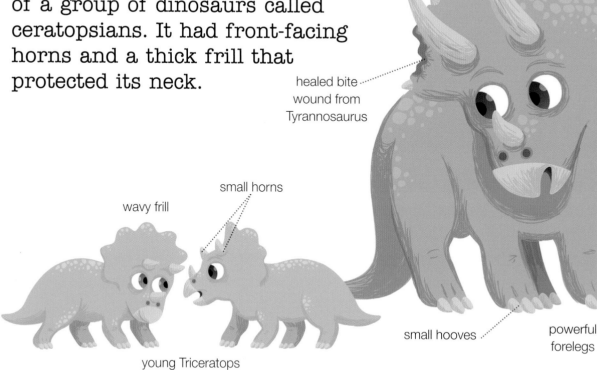

large frill

bony plates

healed bite wound from Tyrannosaurus

small horns

wavy frill

young Triceratops

small hooves

powerful forelegs

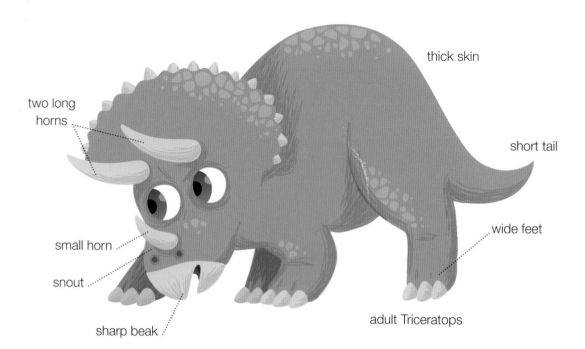

thick skin

two long horns

short tail

small horn

wide feet

snout

sharp beak

adult Triceratops

These dinosaurs belonged to the same group as Triceratops, but they were slightly different.

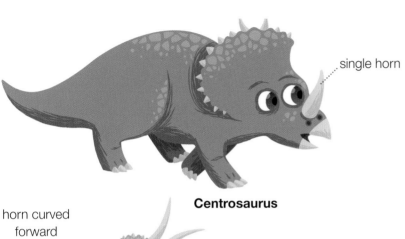

single horn

Centrosaurus

horn curved forward

Einiosaurus

many horns on the frill

long horn on the nose

Styracosaurus

Why
are dinosaur names so complicated

Dinosaurs are given scientific names that usually come from Greek and Latin words. Scientists chose them to describe the animals.

For example, *Triceratops* means "three-horned face." *Baryonyx*: "heavy claw." *Ampelosaurus*: "vineyard lizard."

Baryonyx

When dinosaur fossils were first studied, scientists reconstructed the bones as lizard-like creatures. This dinosaur is *Kentrosaurus*, or "spiky lizard."

Stegosaurus

With big, flat plates along their backs, they are easy to recognize.

two rows
of plates

short
forelegs

long hind
legs

four spikes

rounded
back

walking
slowly

small
head

long snout

Marshosaurus

short, muscular tail

lopping off plants with its beak

Upright and triangular, the plates ran from neck to tail. They were unique and impressive!

These hard, bony plates might have helped a Stegosaurus be recognized by its friends or intimidate an enemy.

The blood circulating inside the plates also warmed or cooled the body.

Ankylosaurus

These peaceful plant-eaters were well protected from hungry predators by their armor.

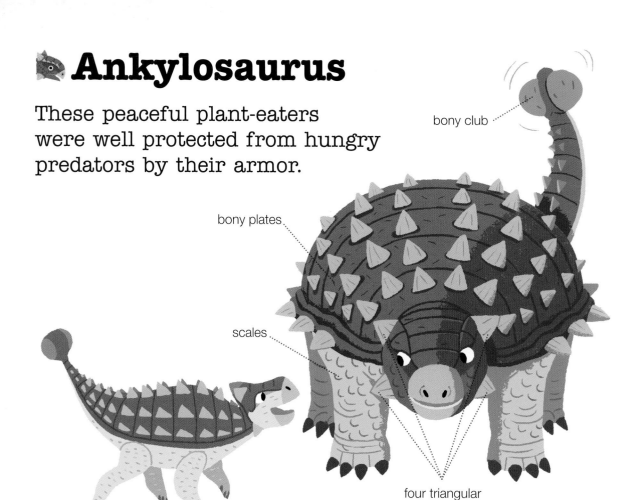

bony club

bony plates

scales

four triangular horns

spikes

heavy, powerful tail

small, leaf-shape teeth

Just like the Ankylosaurus, other members of the ankylosaurian group had armor made of knobs and plates of bone that covered most of their bodies.

Euoplocephalus

Nodosaurus

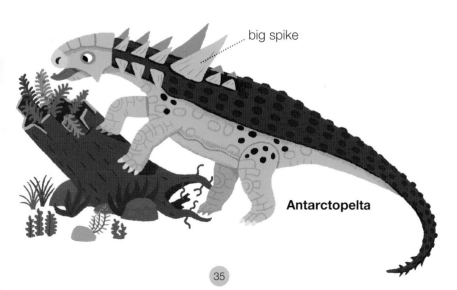

big spike

Antarctopelta

With its suit of armor, the Ankylosaurus looked invincible. It probably was not even scared of the Tyrannosaurus!

The Ankylosaurus was one of the best-protected dinosaurs. But its belly and legs weren't armored. Those were its weak spots.

When it was attacked, it could lie flat on the ground and fold its legs underneath itself—similar to how a turtle can take cover inside its shell.

Iguanodon

When it stood on its hind legs, the Iguanodon was as tall as three humans. It could walk and run on two legs or all four!

ginkgo

standing on hind legs

broad beak

swamp

fern

small hooves

walking on four legs

How
are dinosaurs related to iguanas ?

very sharp
thumb spike

Neovenator

clawing
an enemy

five digits

holding
a branch

Have you ever seen an iguana on TV or at the zoo? It's a large lizard that lives in warm places. Its name sounds like *Iguanodon*.

The Iguanodon's teeth look like an iguana's. And its name even means "iguana tooth."

While dinosaurs and iguanas are reptiles, they both belong to different groups and are only distantly related. Some iguanas can even be pets.

Ancient Reptiles **8**
After the Dinosaurs **70**

Baryonyx

With their crocodile-like heads and sharp teeth, these dinosaurs were perfectly built for hunting fish.

frightened young Iguanodon

lying in wait for prey

long, flat skull

nostril

thin, cone-shaped teeth

powerful forelegs

huge claws

Baryonyx footprints

Titanosaur

crocodile-like snout

scavenging

tearing apart dead prey

river

We don't know what kind of odor dinosaurs gave off. But considering all the fish that Baryonyx ate, it must have smelled a lot like fish!

Depending on where they lived and what they ate, dinosaurs might have had a strong smell, like turtles do.

However, predatory dinosaurs would have had a good sense of smell to locate their prey. Can you recognize foods by their smell?

Velociraptor

The Velociraptor was a small but fast and fierce predator. Its claws were also powerful weapons!

Tylocephale

powerful jaws

jumping onto prey

attacking with claws

many sharp teeth

long, stiff tail

Protoceratops

running
away

long,
flat head

feathers

retractable
claw

long hind
legs

41

There were so many types of dinosaurs: big and slow ones, medium-size ones, small and lighter ones.

The Tyrannosaurus was heavy and not very fast, but it took big steps. The Velociraptor could go as fast as a car in the city!

The Dromiceiomimus would win the race! It belonged to a group of dinosaurs called ornithomimids, which could run about 25 miles (40 kilometers) per hour!

Parasaurolophus

These dinosaurs are easily recognized by their long, tubular crests.

living in a herd

running away

little
Parasaurolophus

long crest

pine
tree

flat duck bill

short
forelegs

short tail

long hind
legs

Tyrannosaurus on the hunt

Saurolophus

Corythosaurus

at rest

What a ruckus! If you could go back in time, you'd hear many different noises. Like all animals, dinosaurs talked to one another.

grrowwwl!

Mooo!

Boh

To make sounds, the Parasaurolophus inflated its cheeks, then sent air through its big crest. That made the sound of its call: *Puuohh!*

Each one had its own call. That way, they could recognize one another from a distance or warn each other about danger. How do you call for help?

Self-defense **52**

Let's Review!

Can you match each of these dinosaurs with the ones in the scenes on the right?

Which of these dinosaurs are part of the ankylosaurian group? Which ones are part of the ceratopsian group?

Match the dinosaur with its body parts below.

Antarctopelta

Parasaurolophus

Iguanodon

Triceratops

Baryonyx

Velociraptor

Diplodocus

Stegosaurus

Tyrannosaurus

Whose legs are these?

Whose spikes are these?

What about these mouths?

Dinosaur
Life

Eating Plants

Dinosaurs that were herbivores spent a lot of time eating all sorts of plants.

grazing on treetops

lopping off a leaf with its beak

araucaria

Hadrosaurus

Brachiosaurus

using its tail for balance

cycads

pine tree

chewing for a long time

Ouranosaurus

Panoplosaurus

Edmontosaurus

cutting a stem with its teeth

Psittacosaurus

bug

Iguanodon

breaking open a seed with its beak

Lesothosaurus

swallowing without chewing

Diplodocus

torn-off branch

Stegosaurus

feeding on the ground

flowers

Hypsilophodon

pine cone

Triceratops

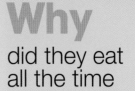
You don't need to catch or gather your own food. Dinosaurs spent nearly all their time looking for plants to eat.

Because of their large size, dinosaurs had to eat a lot of plants for energy.

Can you think of animals today that spend a lot of time eating plants?

Sauropods **14**
The End of the Dinosaurs **68**

⤳ Hunting

Dinosaurs that were carnivores caught and ate other animals.

approaching
its prey

Albertosaurus   **Ankylosaurus**

hunting

weak
Tenontosaurus

Deinonychus

being
hunted

Deinonychus

Acrocanthosaurus

injured
Apatosaurus

catching
a fish

Spinosaurus

hunting large
prey alone

Allosaurus

eating
its prey

Ceratosaurus

Carnivores
sometimes
ate fruits.

catching
a grasshopper

Pelecanimimus

Ornithomimus

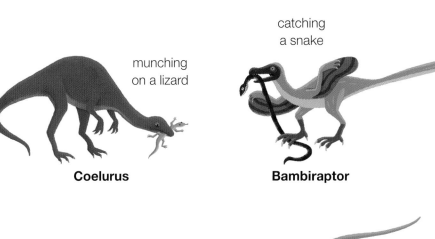

munching
on a lizard

catching
a snake

Coelurus

Bambiraptor

missing
its prey

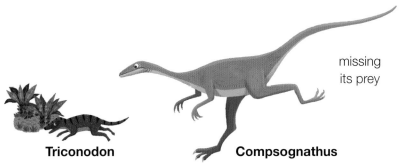

Triconodon

Compsognathus

What
was the life span of dinosaurs

?

You know your own age, but it's hard to know how old dinosaurs were. Often, the bigger they were, the more likely they lived to old age.

Sauropods were very big and fairly peaceful. They might have lived for more than 100 years.

Theropods, as hunters, had rougher lives. They probably lived only to be about 30. Did you know that a human usually lives for about 80 years?

Theropods **12**
Self-Defense **52**

Self-Defense

When they were attacked, dinosaurs had nothing but their bodies to defend themselves.

Albertosaurus

Styracosaurus

Diplodocus

knocking over an enemy with a blow from its tail

stabbing with horns

Allosaurus

threatening the enemy with its spikes

Ceratosaurus

Stegosaurus

striking with
its club-like tail

Gorgosaurus

Ankylosaurus

breaking
an enemy's leg

running away

Tyrannosaurus

Edmontosaurus

living in a group
for protection

protecting
the young

Dromaeosaurus

Centrosaurus

How
did dinosaurs get along

?

Some dinosaurs had no problem living in the same place as others. They all could find enough to eat. They co-existed.

Members of the same group would usually help each other. However, there were fights if several of them wanted to be the boss!

But a Stegosaurus and a Triceratops who were friends? That happens only in stories and cartoons—they lived in different time periods.

Hunting **50**
The Young **56**

♥ Reproduction

To attract female dinosaurs, male dinosaurs would show off their features or fight each other.

Parasaurolophus

short crest

female

long crest

male

calling to the female

Dilophosaurus

small double crest

female

large double crest

male

meeting

Triceratops

female

males

changing the color of their frills

choosing a male

trying to attract the female

Centrosaurus

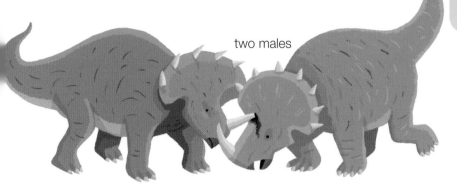

two males

hitting each other
with their horns

Pachycephalosaurus

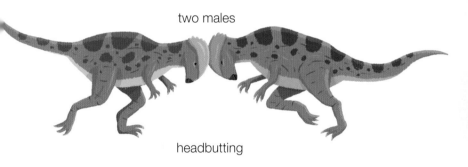

two males

headbutting

male

female

winning the fight
to attract the female

What
were dinosaur families like ?

A daddy and mommy dinosaur living together with their young would be cute! Scientists aren't really sure if that happened.

Scientists think that some dinosaurs lived on their own, but they would meet up with others of their group at various times.

Other dinosaurs lived in herds that included adults and the young. They might have been led by an older dinosaur.

 The Young

After hatching from their eggs, the young grew up fast. The eggs were fragile.

eggs

Oviraptor

Maiasaura

Diplodocus

Velociraptor

Argentinosaurus

Orodromeus

nest dug into sand

laying eggs

Oviraptor

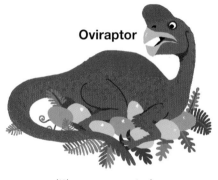

sitting on eggs to keep them warm and safe

Diplodocus

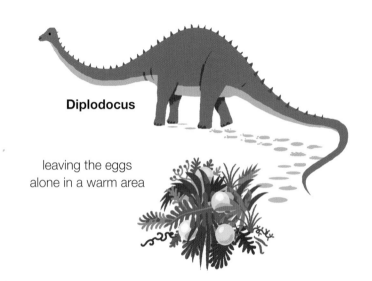

leaving the eggs alone in a warm area

quickly leaving the nest

coming out of the shell

downy covering

newly hatched Troodon

Maiasaura

laying eggs in
a nest as a group

nest of mud

female

male

many
newborns

taking care of
their young

Dromaeosaurus

getting eaten
by a carnivore

stages of growth for a Tyrannosaurus

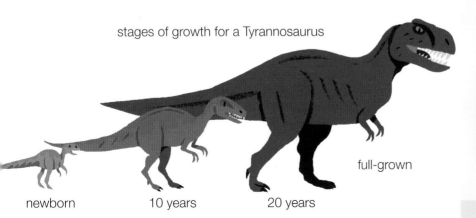

newborn

10 years

20 years

full-grown

When you were a baby, you drank milk, like all mammals do. But dinosaurs were reptiles.

Maiasaura parents would swallow plants, then bring the food back into their mouths when it was feeding time. The babies would eat the mashed-up food.

An Oviraptor parent probably brought dead animals to their young. But many newborns could find food all on their own!

At Night

Not all was calm at night. Dinosaurs made the most of the dark for feeding.

catching small prey

big eyes for seeing in the dark

Troodon on the hunt

Ornithomimus

Bambiraptor on the lookout

Parasaurolophus

sleeping

How

smart were dinosaurs

?

needing to eat
day and night

Styracosaurus

eating
the flowers

Ankylosaurus

To find out, scientists have studied dinosaur skulls and calculated the size of their brains, which is where thinking happens.

Troodon had the biggest brain compared to its body size of all dinosaurs. That might mean that it was very intelligent.

Scientists think the Stegosaurus was one of the least-clever dinosaurs and that its brain worked very slowly.

Eating Plants **48**
Hunting **50**

Let's Review!

Look at these dinosaurs. Which ones were herbivores? Which ones were carnivores?

With the help of these descriptions, match the egg to its dinosaur.

Maiasaura eggs were the
same shape as chicken eggs.

Diplodocus eggs were
completely round.

Velociraptor eggs
were pear-shaped.

Look at these two scenes.
Where are the Deinonychus? What are they doing?
What's happening in each scene?

Can you name any animals that hunt
other animals to feed themselves?
Did you know that some of those hunters
are hunted by even stronger animals?

Life without Dinosaurs

Before the Dinosaurs

Millions of years before dinosaurs appeared, animals lived in water. Some of them eventually became land creatures. The animals shown on these pages lived at various times over a period of about 230 million years.

IN WATER

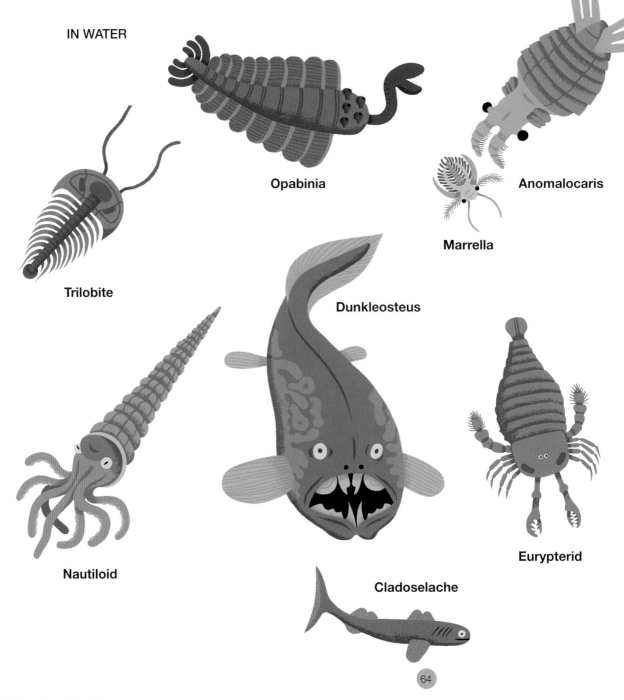

Opabinia

Anomalocaris

Marrella

Trilobite

Dunkleosteus

Nautiloid

Eurypterid

Cladoselache

ON LAND

Hylonomus

Acanthostega

Dimetrodon

Estemmenosuchus

Gorgonopsian

These creatures never crossed paths with dinosaurs. In fact, almost all of them disappeared long before dinosaurs existed.

Boo!

They were killed by natural disasters. They could have drowned in floods, or died because of hot lava and ash from erupting volcanoes.

Fortunately, some animals survived and started to repopulate Earth. Certain members of the reptile family evolved into dinosaurs!

Asteroid Strike

In the time of the dinosaurs, a huge rock from outer space fell from the sky one day.

gigantic asteroid or meteorite

⚡ Disasters

This strike caused a series of deadly disasters for the dinosaurs.

earthquakes

volcanic eruptions

tidal waves or tsunamis

Scientists are like detectives. They study clues to figure out how dinosaurs died.

By studying the remains of the dinosaurs, they found out when the dinosaurs disappeared. They also found rocks that fell from the sky.

Scientists discovered that a crater in Mexico was caused by an asteroid that struck Earth about 66 million years ago. That was when dinosaurs were wiped out.

The End of the Dinosaurs

The catastrophes caused Earth to become dark and cold. Without light, plants and algae died. The dinosaurs that ate them died too. But some living things were able to survive.

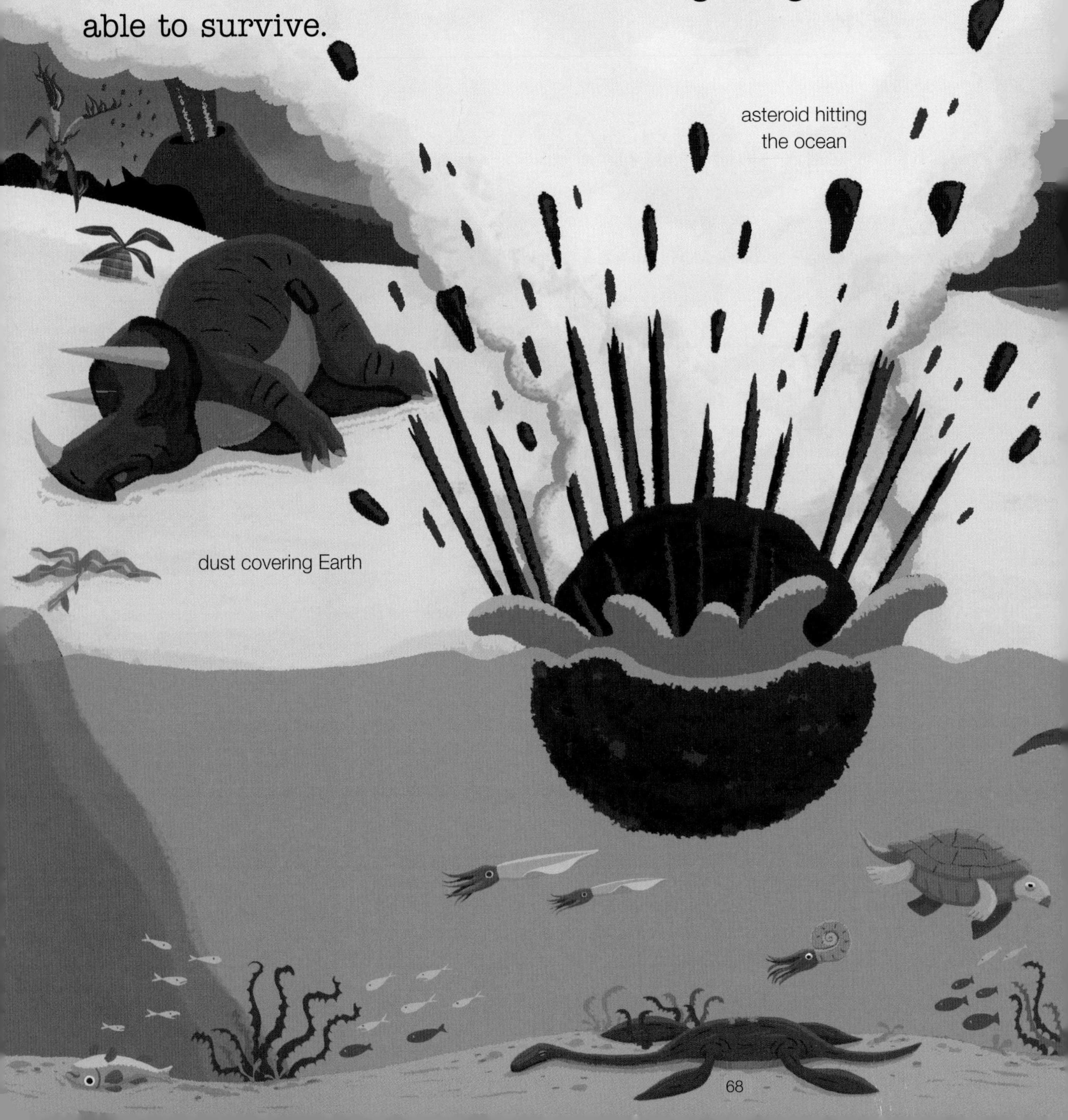

asteroid hitting the ocean

dust covering Earth

68

What
if dinosaurs came back to life ?

ash and dust in the air blocking sunlight

worms going underground

There are movies and stories in which dinosaurs reappear on Earth and find themselves among humans.

Some people dream of using science to bring them back to life. But that's impossible!

What do you think? How would these enormous prehistoric animals live with us in modern times?

Disasters **67** 🌱

From Past to Present **82**

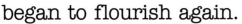After the Dinosaurs

Daylight finally reappeared after thousands of years of darkness. Plant and animal life began to flourish again.

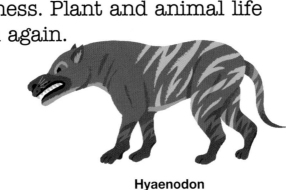

Icaronycteris

Miacis

Hyaenodon

Coryphodon

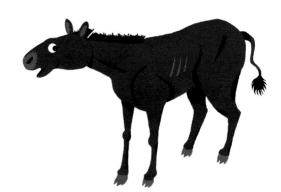

Hyracodon

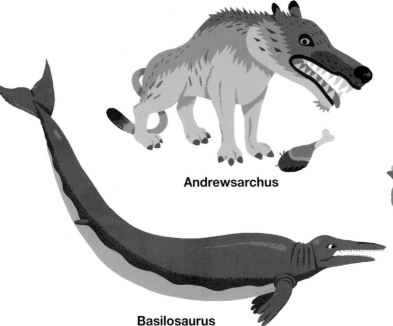

Andrewsarchus

Basilosaurus

Uintathere

Hapalops

Pristichampsus

Gastornis

The Komodo dragon may remind you of a dinosaur, but they are not related.

Birds descended from dinosaurs. Some dinosaurs that could climb started jumping from branch to branch, then began to fly.

It's funny to think that this pigeon has a dinosaur for an ancestor. However, you can find similarities in their clawed feet and scales on their legs.

From Past to Present **82**
Other Animals **90**

Paleontology Dig

Today scientists dig into the ground to uncover fossils, the remains of dinosaurs and other objects.

being careful not to damage the fossil

hammer

scraper

needle

chisel

tweezers

notepad

pneumatic drill

paleontologist

measuring the fossil

cleaning the bone

wheelbarrow full of dirt

fossil of a dinosaur skull

shovel

photographer

brush

packing the fossils

cotton

protecting the fossil

making fossils sturdier with glue

roll of plaster cloth

plaster shell

bucket

crate

🧪 Laboratory

Next the scientists study their finds in a laboratory.

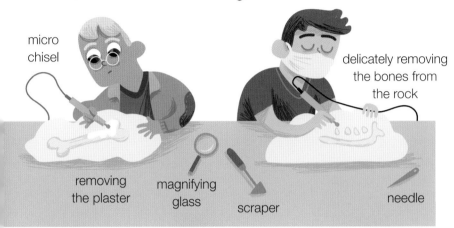

micro chisel

delicately removing the bones from the rock

removing the plaster

magnifying glass

scraper

needle

binocular microscope

ultrasonic cleaner

observing the fossil up close

repairing broken pieces

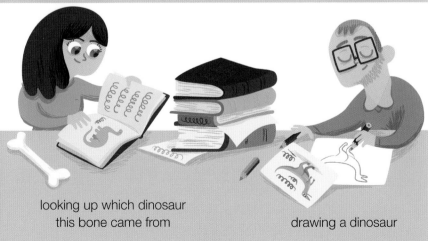

looking up which dinosaur this bone came from

drawing a dinosaur

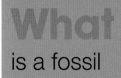
Scientists uncover bones that are as hard as rock. They're trapped in the ground and in several pieces.

A long time ago, a dinosaur died here. It fell into a river. Then it was buried in the riverbed, under many layers of sand and mud.

Millions of years went by, and its bones transformed into rock. Its skeleton is now a fossil for us to discover.

Museum

In this building, you can marvel at collections of reconstructed dinosaurs.

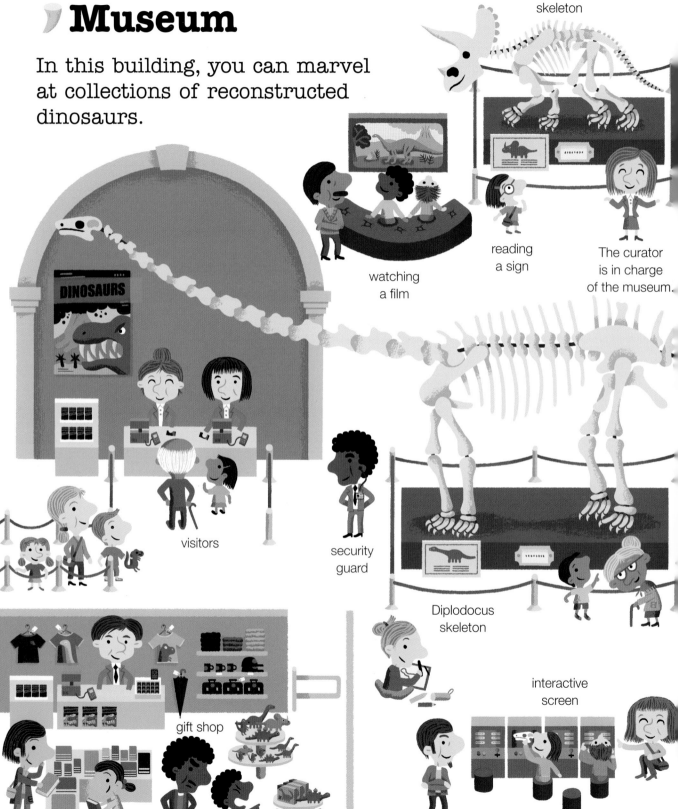

Triceratops skeleton

watching a film

reading a sign

The curator is in charge of the museum.

visitors

security guard

Diplodocus skeleton

gift shop

interactive screen

How

do we know what they looked like **?**

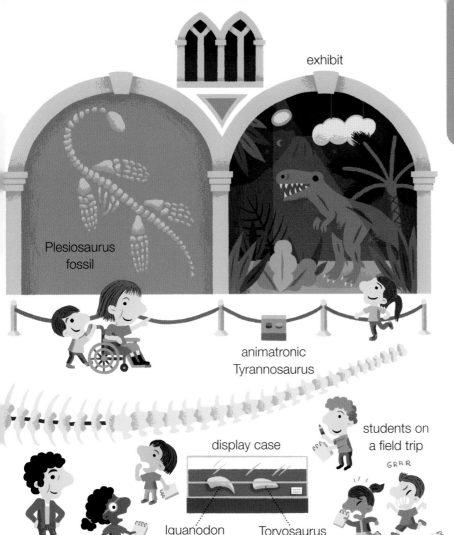

exhibit

Plesiosaurus fossil

animatronic Tyrannosaurus

display case

students on a field trip

GRRR

Iguanodon thumb spike

Torvosaurus claw

paleontology lab

metal frame

reconstructing a Stegosaurus skeleton

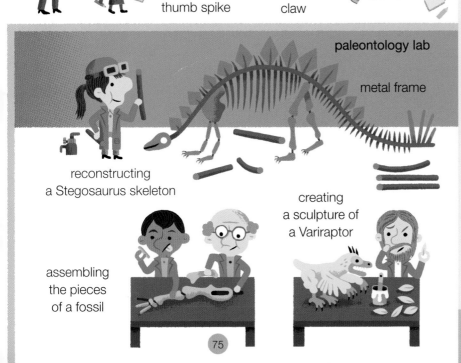

creating a sculpture of a Variraptor

assembling the pieces of a fossil

It's rare to find a complete dinosaur skeleton. Usually the fossil is broken and there are only pieces left. Sometimes soft tissues are found with the fossils.

Paleontologists put the pieces together, like a puzzle. They study the tissue to learn the shape of the muscles that would cover the bones.

It's hard work, and sometimes scientists get it wrong. Here's how they imagined the Iguanodon in the past. Do you see how that's different from the actual dinosaur?

💻 Researchers

There are many jobs that involve studying Earth and its people, plants, and animals in both the past and the present.

Paleontologists study fossilized animals.

Paleobotanists study fossilized plants.

Archaeologists study people and monuments from ancient times.

Science journalists report on scientific discoveries.

Anthropologists study the lives
of groups of people.

Geologists are interested
in Earth and rocks.

Zoologists study
living animals.

Entomologists specialize
in insects.

How

many more dinosaurs are there to find ?

In this book, you learn about a wide variety of dinosaurs. Some are very similar to one another, while others are very different.

We don't know yet all the different types that existed. Paleontologists think there are still hundreds left to discover!

With so many possibilities, what do you think dinosaurs might have looked like?

Outdoor Museum

As you explore this big park, you'll encounter dinosaurs that look and feel real.

information sign

listening dinosaur no

dinosaur statues

fossilized eggs

welcome center

museum map

Tyrannosaurus statue

Iguanodon footprints

picnic tables

Brachiosaurus
skeleton

touching the
Dilophosaurus
statue

paleontology
dig for kids

uncovering
fake fossils

Where
can you find
a dinosaur egg ?

Imagine finding a dinosaur egg on your daily walk or while digging in your garden. That would be so cool!

To actually discover dinosaur bones and fossils, you would have to do a bit of digging. They can be fairly close to the surface.

Sometimes fossils are found by accident during construction, such as when roads are being built.

Paleontology Dig **72**

Museum **74**

Let's Review!

Look at these creatures. Which of them came before the dinosaurs?
Which of them came after?

Do these ancient animals resemble any present-day animals?

Here are three pictures showing what happened right before dinosaurs went extinct.
Put them in the correct order.

It takes a lot of work before a dinosaur skeleton can be shown in a museum.
From discovery to exhibit, put the pictures in the correct order.

Time to play paleontologist!

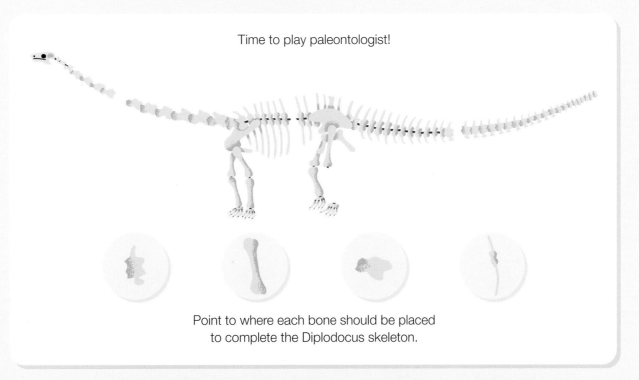

Point to where each bone should be placed
to complete the Diplodocus skeleton.

From Past to Present

Before the Dinosaurs

Nautiloid

Dimetrodon

Herrerasaurus

Acanthostega

Pelecanimimus

Cretaceous Peri

Ouranosaurus

Iguanodon

Deinonychus

Centrosaurus

Parasaurolophus

the asteroid strike

Tyrannosaurus

Ankylosaurus

Pachycephalosaurus

Velociraptor

dinosaurs become extinct

Triassic Period

Coelophysis bauri

Plateosaurus

Jurassic Period

Vulcanodon

Dilophosaurus

Diplodocus

Baryonyx

Compsognathus

Allosaurus

Stegosaurus

Cenozoic Era

woolly mammoth

early humans

present-day humans

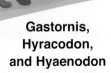

Gastornis, Hyracodon, and Hyaenodon

The Sizes of Dinosaurs

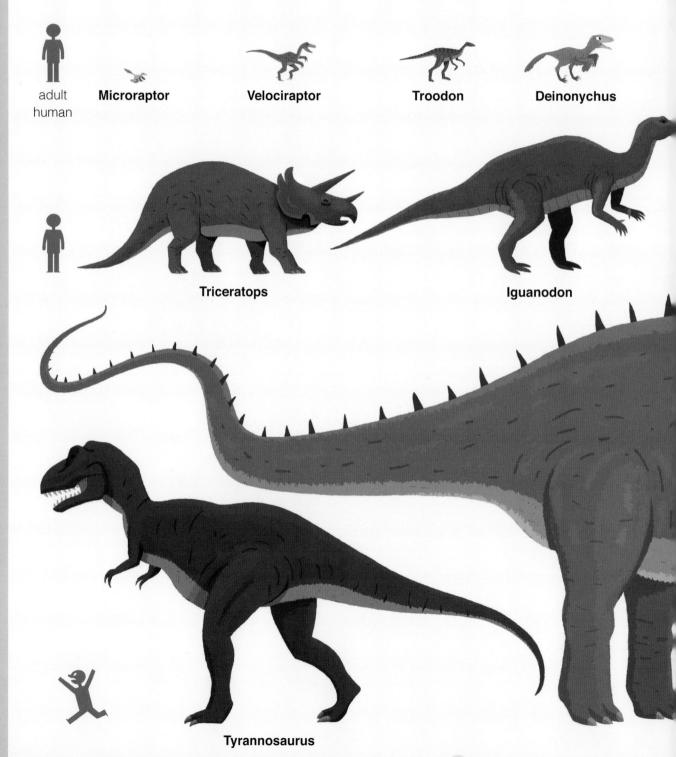

adult
human

Microraptor

Velociraptor

Troodon

Deinonychus

Triceratops

Iguanodon

Tyrannosaurus

Ankylosaurus

Stegosaurus

Baryonyx

Parasaurolophus

Diplodocus

Biggest, Heaviest, and More!

The Argentinosaurus
was the heaviest.

The Anchiornis was one
of the smallest and lightest.

The Brachiosaurus
was one of the tallest.

The Diplodocus hallorum
was one of the longest.

The Ankylosaurus
was among the slowest.

The Dromiceiomimus
was the fastest.

The Pentaceratops had the largest
head in relation to its body.

The Tyrannosaurus
had the biggest teeth.

The Therizinosaurus
had the biggest claws.

The biggest fossilized egg ever
discovered belonged to a sauropod.

The World of Dinosaurs

Here is where scientists have found the remains of dinosaurs.

NORTH
AMERICA

ATLANTIC
OCEAN

PACIFIC
OCEAN

SOUTH
AMERICA

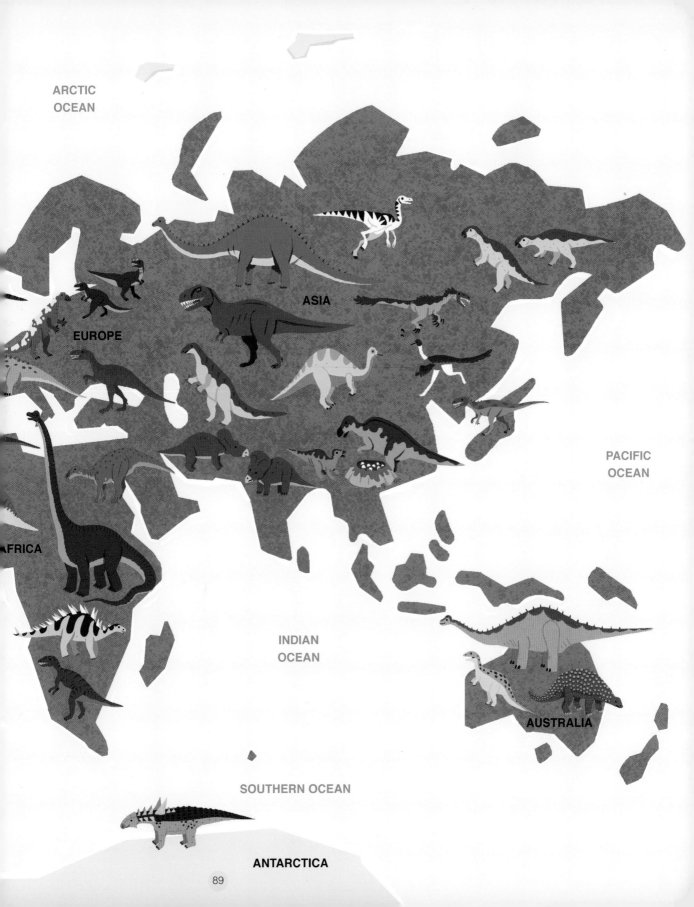

ARCTIC
OCEAN

ASIA

EUROPE

PACIFIC
OCEAN

FRICA

INDIAN
OCEAN

AUSTRALIA

SOUTHERN OCEAN

ANTARCTICA

89

Other Animals

These creatures lived at the same time as the dinosaurs. Some of them still exist today, but their bodies are different.

Pliosaurus

Ichthyosaurus

Plesiosaurus

Mosasaurus

sea crocodile

sea turtle

Hesperornis

shark

ammonite

belemnite

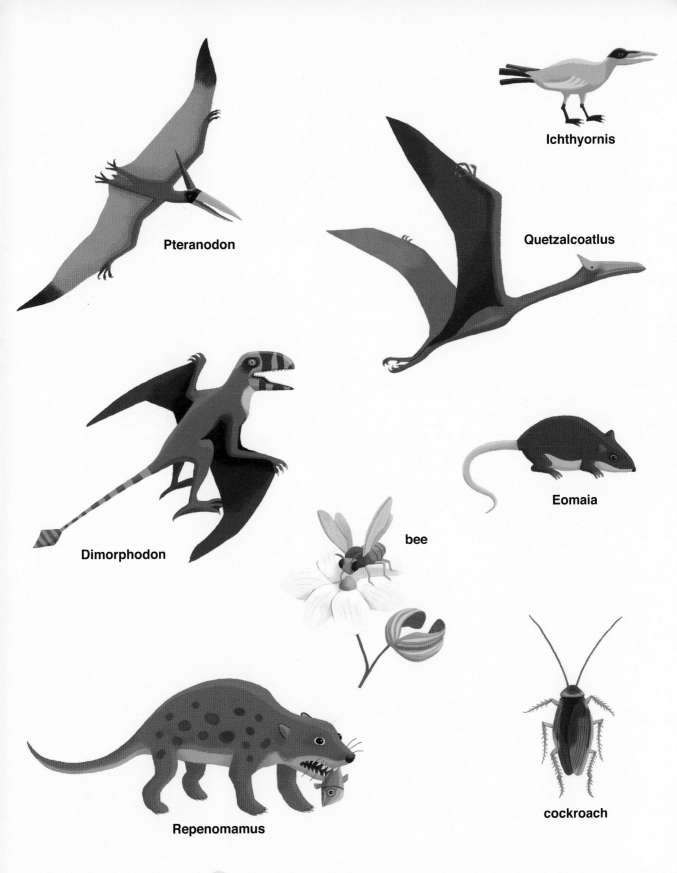

Ichthyornis

Pteranodon

Quetzalcoatlus

Dimorphodon

Eomaia

bee

Repenomamus

cockroach

Index

horn 9, 12, 20, 30, 31, 34, 52, 55
horsetail 27
Huayangosaurus 16
human 83, 84, 85
hunting 28, 29, 43, 50–51, 58
Hyaenodon 70, 83
Hylonomus 65
Hypsilophodon 49
Hyracodon 70, 83

I

Icaronycteris 70
Ichthyornis 91
Ichthyosaurus 90
iguana 37
Iguanodon 18, 19, 36–37, 38, 48, 75, 78, 82, 84
Indian Ocean 89

J

jaw 8, 28, 40
jumping 40
Jurassic 26, 83

K

Kentrosaurus 17, 31

L

laboratory 73
Lambeosaurus 9
laying eggs 56
leg 8, 11, 19, 20, 29, 30, 32, 36, 38, 41, 42
Leptoceratops 21
Lesothosaurus 48
life span 51
lizard 10, 31, 37, 51
lying in wait 29, 38

M

magnifying glass 73
magnolia 29
Maiasaura 18, 56, 57
Mamenchisaurus 15
Marginocephalian 20
Marrella 64
Marshosaurus 33
measuring 72
meat 12, 29
Melanorosaurus 11
meteorite 66
Miacis 70
micro chisel 73
Microraptor 13, 84
microscope 73
Mosasaurus 90
museum 74–75, 78–79

N

Nautiloid 64, 82
neck 9, 14, 15, 16, 27, 28, 30
needle 72, 73
Neovenator 37
nest 18, 56, 57
Nodosaurus 35
North America 28, 88
nostril 14, 38

O

oak tree 28
observing 73
odor 39
Opabinia 64
Ornithomimus 51, 58
ornithopod 18–19
Orodromeus 56
Ouranosaurus 18, 48, 82
Oviraptor 13, 56, 57

P

Pachycephalosaurus 20, 55, 82
Pacific Ocean 88, 89
paleobotanist 76
paleontologist 72, 75, 76, 77
Panoplosaurus 17, 48
Parasaurolophus 42–43, 54, 58, 82, 85
Pelecanimimus 51, 82
Pentaceratops 87
photographer 72
pine cone 49
pine tree 42, 48
Pisanosaurus 10
plant 15, 16, 17, 26, 27, 28, 29, 33, 36, 42, 48, 49, 57, 68, 76
plaster 72, 73
plate 16, 17, 30, 32, 33, 34
Plateosaurus 11, 83
Plesiosaurus 75, 90
Pliosaurus 90
pneumatic drill 72
prey 28, 38, 40, 50, 58
Pristichampsus 71
protecting 72
protection 21, 53
Protoceratops 21, 40
Psittacosaurus 20, 48
Pteranodon 91

Q

Quetzalcoatlus 91

R

repairing 73
Repenomamus 91
resting 43
retractable claw 41
river 39
running away 41, 42, 53

S

sail 9, 18
Saurolophus 43
sauropod 14–15, 26, 51, 87
scale 34, 71
scavenger 28, 39
science journalist 76
scientist 72, 73, 76
scraper 72
sculpture 75
Scutellosaurus 17
sea crocodile 90
sea turtle 90
seed 48
self-defense 52–53
sequoia 26
shark 90
shovel 72
sitting on eggs 18, 56
size 13, 15, 41, 59, 84–85
skeleton 73, 74, 75, 79
skin 8, 9, 30
skull 21, 38
skull cap 20
sleeping 58
smell 39
snake 51
snout 30, 32, 39
sound 43
South America 88
Southern Ocean 89
speed 41
spike 9, 16, 17, 20, 32, 34, 35, 37, 52, 75
spine 26
Spinosaurus 9, 50
statue 78
Stegosaurus 32–33, 49, 52, 59, 75, 83, 85
Styracosaurus 31, 52, 59
surviving 68
swamp 36